Where My Umbilical Is Buried

Sundress Publications • Knoxville, TN

ISBN: 978-1-951979-43-0
Library of Congress Control Number: 2022951074
Published by Sundress Publications
www.sundresspublications.com

Editor: Tierney Bailey
Managing Editor: Tennison S. Black
Editorial Assistant: Kanika Lawton
Editorial Interns: Fox Auslander, Solstice Black

Colophon: Text set in Bell MT
Cover Design: Kristen Ton
Cover Art: "Florecitas En Mi Corazón" by Stephanie Gonzalez
Author Photo: Mar Mizunaka
Book Design: Sherrel McLafferty

Where My Umbilical Is Buried

Amanda Galvan Huynh

CONTENTS

Two Bodies Breaking Away

For the Resio and Galvan family.
Siempre con amor.

The Songs of Brujería

La Luna would be the brightest on Saturday nights
      for a quince, a wedding, or some other reason
           to celebrate—to fill a dance hall:
      tías refilling plates with barbeque

and gossip. Beer bottles humming
      around mouths. Children playing tag
           under tables until drunk abuelos trap them
      into norteña-ing their boots along to the breath

of el acordeón. When cumbia whisked her way
      through the speakers, the women would line
           the floor to sway in rhythm to *Baila*
      Esta Cumbia. An invitation to *mueve la cintura*

to the music in their blood. These were the songs
      of brujería and this was where the women
           in my family practiced. These were the nights
      my mother would take me onto the dance floor

with her long black hair cumbia-ing to its own beat.
      She would teach me how to listen to the magic
           found in those nights—as if all I had
      to do was press my ear to my pulse—to find my way home.

A Halo of Blue Flames

Before My Mother Was Born

before she was born
her dad died in an
accident except it
wasn't an accident at
least that's what her
brother says he was
twelve at the time but
said their dad was shot
in the fields while
working maybe over
drugs or something
but they shot him
then they turned his
tractor on let it run
over his body her
brother said there
were a lot of gashes
you could see them at
the funeral service
that's what he says
she was not there
she was not born yet
still resting in the
womb but there are
nights she dreams
those gashes feel
like the fields she
works in every day

Portrait of a Daughter and her Mother in a Cotton Field

Floydada, Texas

She remembers the breath
of the sun laboring her skin

until she blended into the earth.
Her mamá ahead racing

empty bags and the clouds—
córrele, before the day's whistle.

One day: my mother on the ground,
her hands' roots unhinged.

Brothers told her *Levántate*
or else she'd get belted. No time

to pick the dirt speckled
in her fleshy knees, or to nurse

the cuts interrupting the life
line of her palm; each fist-sized

cloud blushed in her caked hands.
But she remembers her mamá

most: so far in front of her
that she's the size of her thumb,

the orange bandana tied around
her head swaying with each

movement. Her mamá too busy
picking as much as she could—

she didn't notice. My mother: waiting,
her small body stood still, for her

mamá to look back—even though
my mother knew she couldn't.

Her Family Moves

when the weather changes. From Mathis

    to Lubbock, the sunrise waits

        for the car. It doesn't touch

    the bundled clothes in boxes

and plastic bags. It doesn't know

    that there's no room

        for her First Communion dress

    or that she hides her white

ribbon bow in her pocket.

        From Lubbock to Amarillo

        Mamá's voice rattles

    through the hallway

with no heat, strips the mattress

    of its sheets, and pushes them

        out to the car. Their breath

    fogs the windows until it blurs

out the moon. From Amarillo

to Corpus, her notebooks

crumple as Mamá stuffs blankets

into her backpack. She piles

crates into the trunk, replaces

her doll with a bag of pans.

From Corpus to Mathis, the cops

invite themselves in. She holds

her baby brother's bruised body

as the flesh of their apartment tears.

Four pairs of clean chones

and the wind. It never matters

if it's in the middle of the night

or early in the morning,

or if they are pulled out of school

around noon. They get used to—

When She Asks Her Brother About Their Dad

I lost my first tooth then.

Like I told you

I don't remember
                much. Our dad
was just a mean man.
                If he wasn't working,
he was drinking: the cerveza
                became his left hand.

One time I tripped over his boots
        and as I stood up he hit me
against the wall,
                brushed his boots
off.

When Ma found out
                he had another family—

she kicked him out
        and when he asked if I wanted to go
with him
        or stay,

I stayed.

First Time She Interrupted Mamá

The first time she interrupted Mamá
she was talking with her sisters
in the kitchen. Arroz simmered

in its tomato juice; the blood smeared
between her legs was brighter. She thought
I'm dying at thirteen. She thought *I will die*

if Mamá sees these stains. Blooms
in her shorts. Fear cut into the laughter
like hands caught in the stove's flame.

Mamá uncrossed her arms and followed
her back to the bathroom. With one arm
Mamá reached under the sink. In the cracked

mirror her questions never left her mouth:
Am I sick? Will I bleed forever? What do
I do with all this blood? Am I dying?

Mamá handed her a square wrapped in pink
but didn't explain. *Did your brothers touch you?*
She stared at Mamá's face, calm but impatient.

She tried to figure out what she meant by
touch. *Did your brothers touch you there?*
She shook her head. Mamá nodded, closed

the cabinet. *Put that in your chones.* Mamá
shut the door behind her, the kitchen's noise
rose, and she never interrupted her again.

CPS

Abilene, Texas

She wasn't young enough
to forget the small sound
of her shoelace tip against
the hospital floor. Each click
her own second hand on her
inner clock. She lost count
after two thousand sixty-eight.

Our tíos will be here soon,

her brother patted her. Tías
had heard about Mamá's Lupus
flare up. They had heard
they'd be waiting for them, all
six of them with one bag
of clean clothes. All of them
stretched out on the lobby chairs.

Our tíos will be here soon.

Her stomach tried to digest
emptiness—sopa half-cooked
on the stove. No money for snacks.
When the doctor came to speak
to the family his white coat turned
in the air confused to find children.
The oldest brother told him,

Our tíos will be here soon.

A white nurse came to ask
when their father would arrive.
They held air in their hands—
they had no father who smelled
of dirt. Every hour a nurse came
and walked away. Whispered:
fieldworkers. Neglected.

Our tíos will be here soon.

She dreamed of bowls full of shells,
the smell of onions and chicken
bouillon cubes. She dreamed she saw
Mamá with her bracelets chiming—
until she woke to a woman with singing
bracelets. The woman told them to come
and they did. Even though she told her:

Our tíos will be here soon.

Notes on Absence
Abilene, Texas

1

2

3

4

1 The last photo of Mamá: a blue and pink plaided summer top,
  short blonde hair, a thin gold watch around her left wrist,
  a small panda bear under her arm with a Six Flags map, yellow
  cotton candy in hand, and no smile. The photo doesn't capture
  the smell of her hairspray and sweat. The pace of her breath.

  The words she said right after the photo was taken: .
2 My mother doesn't remember who cleaned out Mamá's cosmetics.
3 Her brothers thumbed coin holes at the arcade, laundromats,
  payphones, and vending machines. No father. No family
  willing to help cover the funeral. They managed to have her body

  transported home. Houston to Abilene. The five of them gathered
4 items to sell. They searched the kitchen tiles, their jean pockets,
  the backs of dressers, the loose ends of rugs and carpets,
  the corners of closets, and under mattresses. They searched
  until they knew how many seams kept them together.

Who La Llorona Cries For

I imagine my mother saw the two blue lines

        as handcuffs made from rivers.

    Twenty-one and pregnant.

    The two blue lines applauding, announcing to her
        in-laws that she had made their son
                a father.
                   Finally.

      Did she think of her mother?

Throughout the next nine months, did she wonder
    if her mother sat outside on the porch
        eating sardines? Did she want to ask
           her how she carried a pond in her belly?

          Or what death felt like at thirty-six?

    In the delivery room, I can hear my mother:
     ¡Ah, mi Mamá—
       calling over
       and over
        —mi Mamá!

          Every contraction,
            a protest, a reason

     not to deliver:
      not to become her mother,

a single mother,

a mother who would leave
                her sixteen-year-old daughter.

In those first seconds I came up for breath

        my mother was already calling for the dead.

Día de la Dama Rubia

The day I saw Catrina my mother and I
were in a car accident. On the sidewalk:

she stood with a crown of red blossoms,
her dress gold, her clavicles exposed

to the pulsing lights of the firetruck. Beside her
a woman: a shrub of blonde hair, penciled

eyebrows, gray bags under her eyes,
and a thin mouth. In my mouth the taste

of quarters, a pulse, a busted lip, split
like tree roots cracking concrete. Front seat.

No seatbelt. *You're lucky you didn't go through
the window.* But willow branched arms bundled

my body for impact, hummed like bees, and tucked
me down onto the car floor. The smell of summer

sweat and tree bark clung onto my brown curls
before someone pulled me awake; set me down

beside bystanders. The red blossoms and blonde
hair slipped down into cracks rivering asphalt—

I never saw Catrina again. I only found the woman's
face in my mother's jewelry box: a tear climbing

her arm, fingertips reaching for the black sleeve
of her blouse, a crease through her right eye,

and her thin mouth. My mother doesn't talk
about this woman or why her mouth looks

like hers. She doesn't talk about the car accident
or if she saw her too—if she can still feel her pulse.

The Nurse

I asked my mother about her mother:
      What did your mom do?

      She was a nurse.

I saw a slender woman in scrubs,
hair tucked into a cap, a woman
working double shifts to place rice
and beans on the table. She was
strong, intelligent; a myth.

As I grew my questions became specific:
      What kind of nurse was she?

      She was never a nurse. She had
      a profession we're not proud of.

I dress my grandmother in hand-me-down
clothes instead of scrubs. I erase the double
shifts and security. I reason with myself—
of course, she couldn't have been a nurse.

Of course:

my grandmother, a single parent,

      saving stale candy apples from the trash
      to bring home to her children,

      bringing her children into the sun
      to pick onions for nickels,

shoveling stale bread into a bag for survival.

When there were no jobs, she gave the rest
she had; her body for a portion of the rent.
My mother doesn't make eye contact

with me as she cannot say the truth
lining the inside of her mouth—
the same one her mother gave her.

Empty Bottles and Beer Cans

The night was crisp with a cumbia beat
climbing up with drunk cigarette smoke.
Men's laughter covered a woman's voice
and a borracho's flush. The gravel gave
into our footsteps as my mother hurried
me to our run-down car. The yelling grew
a mouth of thunder. *Stay here,* she lifted me
into the back, closed the door. *Leave them
alone,* my father's whispers chased after her.
My eyes followed her shadow and I slid
to the other side to line my fingers along
the bottom of the window. Over cars
my tío's cowboy hat hovered in the heat
as my tía's rings held up the night. Voices
muddled by the bass's drum. His body grew
louder. A car shook, un grito. The gravel
gave into her body, a scramble, a pulse
of beats. My father: gone. My mother: wind
against my tío's shirt. His hat upside down
on the ground. A stampede of callused hands
tearing him away. Boots pulled back to music
and another cerveza. His hat dusted off.
A bottle discarded. Her body—picked up.

You Have To Be Ready

when they are—
my mother hands me
        dishes to wash—
even when you're not.
        I watch her turn

the faucet on,
        my hands heat
under the water
        and I wonder
who told her

        to be open
twenty-four/seven.
        How many times
did she lie, split
        open, reviewing

a list of things to be
        done tomorrow?
Did she learn
        over the years:
where to kiss,

        when to touch,
how to suck to make
        her husband finish
quick—to end
        the chore. To make

sure he doesn't drift
      into another
woman's body—
         to say yes—
to make more time

      to be the good wife,
the one who makes floorboards
      reflect the moon
when it comes in
      through the window.

Where is my Mexican Mother?

There's a shell of her haunting
  our house. She has exchanged
    her comadres for gringas. Shoos
the mutts away and welcomes
  the bred dogs to shit in her yard.

    She uncurls her hair
and turns off the Tejano
  music inside her. She's forgotten
    how to cumbia, how to make
tortillas, simmer arroz y frijoles.

  Her ears have gone deaf to Spanish.
    She hires Mexicans to mow her lawn,
for Mexicans to clean her house,
  and holds Pampered Chef parties
    for the neighbors. She stocks

her cabinets with white sugar, highlights
  her hair with blonde, and comes for me.
    A flat iron in one hand to straighten
the Mexicana in me because a white woman
  cannot have a Mexican for a daughter.

Wings Dusted in Dirt

The First Language
after Kimiko Hahn

is not scientific
so the med student does not pronounce
but sings "for-mal-de-hi-de"
in staccato quarter notes.
In her mouth, her tongue realigns
to change her image. To brush away
the recollections of her grandpa,
a Spanish-English dictionary by his bed.
You could cry for his avocado tree
and his junkyard.
The other working hands
brought his wife soda cans
and metal scraps off the road.
The nickels glistened
in their palms.
He couldn't speak to you
though he said *mi nieta*
and patted you on the cheek
as if you were five generations pulled away
saying *grandpa* instead of abuelo.
It occurs to you
that only in America
you will lose
abuelo.

Willie's Junkyard
Floydada, Texas

I used to flatten cans
into stepping stones,
collect screws as coins,
measure my height
with braided metal
strips in the fence,
scavenge Coke tabs
to create bracelets, tilt
empty beer bottle caps

as teacups for dolls,
and gather toys
with missing arms.
I'd carve my name
into abandoned school
desks until I almost
perfected the *Galvan.*
I can count on one hand
the number of times

I went to the junkyard;
the boys went cada día.
Y hoy Abuelo grabs
his jacket and gun—
waves to them a *Vamos.*
Never motions to me.
Never asks if I'd like
to go—to gather shells
of memories never made.

Cicada Shells

I try to regrow
the cut tree

beside the tornado
shelter. Its height,

the bark, the weather
worn spots. I try

to grow its branches
back. The ones

that extended
into a wish-

bone. For three
summers, my only

wish was to climb
into its mouth,

sit in the groove
but I'd be left

on the ground
with blisters

circled in my palms.
One afternoon

you watched
as my arms

realized where
I wanted to go,

pulled me up
so I could see

the top of the stop
sign on the corner.

I saw you sitting
in your wheelchair.

I saw myself
surrounded

by cicada shells
ghosting

the branches.
Translucent

remains quivering
with a breeze,

dipping in and out
of the sunlight

as the leaves pushed
and pulled shade

over their bodies.
I saw myself jump

down, feathering dirt,
to bring you one

so carefully chosen.
You and your smile

with back teeth
missing, a skillet-

cackled laugh,
the way your fingers

rooted into palms,
skin giving in

to the wind
like laundry

on the line. I see
your wheelchair

empty on the porch;
a shell caught

between the sun's
light and shade.

Elegy for las Manos de Mi Abuelo

These workers, they have chosen this way of life
and if they were not happy they would not be here.
— Jack Pandol, *Grower*

they are born
        soft as cotton
                small but able
        to wrap around a stem

they learn to grow
        with each season
                and drift like pollen
        they learn to callus

along the edges
        learn to live with dirt
                under the nails
        they learn to birth

onions from the earth
        cradle peppers away
                from the vine
        break cucumbers free

hands moving
        from Robstown to Mathis
                to El Valle to Floydada
        never finding a place

to rest
        they long to rest
                beside a local girl
       to make a home

they dream of afternoons
        empty of fields
                of cotton
      of soil

they grasp at words
        they cannot read
                for a pencil to shape
       their name

Tongue Untethered
after Melissa Lozada-Oliva

My Spanish spoons the crescent
of my dreams. Her feet walk inside ripples
of a dress sewn with starlight. She holds
my face to untether my tongue from its root
of self-doubt, and leads me into the dark
reflection of the sky. Here, we run—
we run among an uproar of words sprouting:
camino, luna, estrella, casa, calle, coche—
until cities overgrow in my mouth.
People and places I longed to hear
become clear as ice melting in the heat
of a Texas night. My Spanish braids summers
full with fieldwork—her old fingers moving
back and forth tell secretos of spices y ganas—
through the frizz and curls of my Mexican
hair. She tells me, *Qué linda.* She tells me,
Tu nombre es una canción. My name, a song
when I say it in Spanish: Amanda! Those "A"s
shaken free from English, open their arms
to envelop the *Bidi Bidi Bom Bom* mi familia
sways to. My Spanish turns over memories
half understood: dancing norteña con mi abuelo.
The beer on his breath, his boots shuffling,
and the scruff of a farmer's accent. My Spanish
helps me collect Abuelo's words into a jar—
baila, mijita, cerveza, ojalá, trabajo, algodón—
like bits of metal in a junkyard. I press them
to my ear, to hear the worn leather of his voice:

¿Qué pa-hó mija?
                    'stá bien mijita.
          O-ha-la.

My Spanish cracks open these lines to show me
the softness between las palabras, the untranslatable
in expressions, the pieces I feel are missing
from my whole. My Spanish stays until dawn quiets
the night, asks for me to sing my name into the sun—
because she does not want to forget its music.

Where My Umbilical Is Buried
Abilene, Texas—circa 1989 - 1995

Do our bellies remember
the sound of two bodies

breaking away?

My mother waited two weeks
for my umbilical cord to dry.

Like a rose stem
she pruned it, wrapped

the curled flesh in cloth,
tucked it beside her dead

Mamá's necklace, and waited
for our own home with roots:

a corner one, two bedrooms,
and a kitchen in need of repair.

I can't remember the street name.

I only see shadows of the house.

The backyard fence,
a wall of cinderblocks,

my secret garden
with patchy grass,

a metal swing set,
a clothesline,
one tree—

my father promised
he'd build a tree-
                house
with a hook
for piñatas.

I bit my little cousin on the stomach
for her piñata candy.

My time-out corner was in the dining room.

Small scuff marks on the floorboards,
thirty minutes felt like a whole afternoon
of swinging with my shadow. I would whisper
songs into the wall and wonder if it was lonely too.

Did our bellies stand at the edges of walls
waiting to be taken back
into flesh?

Under the table's left rib, I drew my name in pink crayon and a heart in purple.

I'd add to my Sistine table whenever adult legs lined the chairs—when they jumped and fiddled. I learned "cut the deck" could not be done with a karate chop. Ugly beans were for Lotería. Tornadoes of laughter could not break down our walls.

Where is that table?

Is my name

still waxed

in pink?

I'd twist my mother's lipstick until the pink was the tallest,
press my lips into it the way I thought she did, cover my mouth
and chin, then squish the beauty back into the tube.

My ruins:

Pink Parfait
Rubellite
Bois de Rose
Maple Sugar
Rosa Rosa

Time-out corner was in the dining room—
on impatient days I'd be belted.

My *Beauty and the Beast* sheets were always being washed.
I'd wet the bed. I'd wake up. I'd wet the bed. I'd wake up.
I'd wet the bed. I'd be belted. I'd wet the bed. I'd be belted.
I'd wet the bed. I'd wake up

                             crying.

                             I'd wake up
                                 to the hallway light.

                             Once I woke in the middle
                             of the hallway light's hum.
                             By chance my father came
                             to check on me. He tucked
                             me back into pan dulce
                                         dreams.

                             Once I woke in the middle
                             of the hallway light's hum
                             and waited for him

                             and waited

                                   and waited

                             and

on cold nights, we'd leave the stove on:
a halo of blue flames in the dark.
I was never lost.

On the kitchen counter I learned:
numbers in English,
in Spanish,
flour didn't taste like sugar,
tortillas couldn't be cooked without being flattened,
onions could make you cry if you were jealous.

I never noticed that we were

just getting by.

During the day, my mother took care of white children. I
pretended the little boy was my brother. I would ask her why

I didn't have blonde hair like him or

        Cinderella

                    Smurfette

        Sleeping Beauty

                    Alice

      the girl across the street

                    her mother

      who didn't like me

I played   by myself,

pretending I had

      a brother
      a sister
      a baby

on the way
       lost

on the way
       lost
          lost

I found a baby
     bird, its wings dusted
         in dirt, on a bed
   of leaves—
I cradled its unopened eyes
     in the nest
         of my hands—
     returned the tiny wings.

The last trip to the hospital—
we carried nothing

home.

Does the body remember tethering to its own ocean?

A sky in shades of purple?

A constant wave of pulse?

A boy was supposed to be born in April.
Instead, we put our home in boxes.

I stood at the gate.
  The swings waved

    with a creak.

My father never built a treehouse.

  Would having two children have called him to?
      Would having a son?

          Was I not enough?

I sat in the car.
  The naked tree still

    with the yard, empty.

  If my parents die, how long will it take
      to find the house? To find the tree
          on Woodard Street?

The day the baby bird fell:

I almost mistake
the sound as a fallen

pebble—a gray lost
in patches of yellow

green. Its lungs claw
for air before it chirps.

My father bags cut grass.

My mother kneels
under the tree.
Her hand moves

down its flare, rests
between two roots.
She unearths

the earth
to tuck my flesh in—
hoping

I learn to dig
into the soil
and hold on.

DFW to LAX

As I feel the wheels let go,
       the lady behind me speaks
to her daughter—her voice

like the grind of a molcajete—
       like my abuela's. Both
fluent in Spanglish with a dash

of long 'Ah' sounds in understanding.
       Texas stretches beneath us
the way I rolled dough into Texas-

shaped tortillas with my child-
       sized hands. Papas y huevos
in the air and a pile of toasted

tortillas. One spoonful of breakfast
       could fit in my state-shaped
tortillas but she always let me make them,

pack them for Abuelo's lunch. Abuelo
       always working at the junkyard.
Migrant to his bones he drove across

Texas while she stayed still and centered.
       She never climbed into the belly
of a plane. No desire to—the woman

quiets and the ground has become
       stitches of color, farmland
and roads harder to outline. It blurs

together, and I wonder if I can see
        Floydada from up here or if we
even fly near the town—where I know

Abuelo sits at the table alone—where
        Abuela will never see how close
I lean to the window—trying to find her.

Two Bodies Breaking Away

Before I Was Born

my mother's father
died in an accident
except it wasn't an
accident at least that's
what my mother says
her words are pieces
of fields, tractors,
gunshots, and gashes
my mother's father
died before she was
born before I was
formed her mother
died when my mother
was only sixteen in
Houston in some
hospital she cannot
recall the name lost
her mind doesn't let
her remember she
doesn't search for a
death certificate she is
stuck in the revolving
door of the funeral in
the revolving door of
October sunsets and
wind the revolving
door of fragmented
promises and loose
change but these are
things I only hear I
was not there I was not
born yet still an idea

hidden in her flesh
listening to her heart
beat into cold cramped
rooms and on cracked
nights I found her in
her dreams in fields
looking for her mother

Verses

I fear the words my mother has trouble spelling;
using *t-h-e-i-r* when she really means *t-h-e-r-e*
or *your* when she means *you're*. I see her
in the study sounding out a word, typing
then retyping but never able to make the red
underline disappear. I'm ten and she calls me
to check her spelling—*How do you spell appreciate?*
She pronounces the word, *ah-pre-key-ate*.
I correct her, but my mouth carries the hesitation
of her tongue, of her fragmented education, the belief
that intelligence is hereditary. Before bed, I repeated
letter and leather to teach my tongue the difference.
I practiced writing verses of the bible to teach
myself the difference in myself versus her.

To Climb Up Güera
after Gloria Anzaldúa

My Latina friend confesses:
I was afraid of you—
    that you were one of those Latinas—
you know the ones.

I know the ones standing under
my high school's stairwells cutting
    fifth period, who know how to graffiti
their notebooks in Chicano, who call me

whitewashed, who know my tongue
is not Chicana enough for their ears.
    There's not enough slang in four years
of high school Spanish to understand

that *'stá bien mija* means *Está bien mi hija.*
It is not enough to have Spanish-speaking parents
    who have left their tongues on the front porch
of their family's small migrant houses

because those lives were not enough
for their own dreams. Dreams that could not live
    in a one-bedroom house with too many bodies
turning the living room into a dining room

for dinner, and into the children's room
in time for dreams—my parents' dreams shed
    the dirt, the calluses, the boots, the tongue
for the suburban life. The chalk outline of squared

lawns, unbroken sidewalks, well-dressed kids,
and schools with white teachers. With white walls,
    white students, whiteboards, white paper—
white stairs for me to hide underneath.

Letter to My First Gold Hoops

You came in a white box
pillowed on pink. Your body
the width of my finger, a shell

pattern tracing the curve
of your sonrisa. I can see
my mother over the glass

choosing you: her own hoops
glinting in the light. She tucked
you in her purse and brought you

home to me. On my fifth birthday,
she slid you through the holes
of my ears and you dangled

beside my brown curls. You took
in the world above my shoulders—
learned to swim, ate elotes and searched

for old dresses at the flea market,
sat through First Communion, read
books on road trips across Texas,

made tortillas with Abuela, climbed
onto buses for first days of school—
to you this was our forever—

but middle school taught me
the word *wetback*. Taught me
the place of my skin. Curly hair

should be straightened. Dyed.
Colored contacts should cover
the earth in my eyes. Taught me

how to unclasp you from my flesh,
to choose silver over gold, and leave
the pride of you on my dresser.

Eschúchame cuando digo: I'm sorry
for ever hiding your sonrisa—
when all you wanted was to love.

When My Little Sister Mistakes Selena for Selena Gomez

I whip around so fast she gets whiplash. No sister
of mine will confuse Selena with Selena Gomez.
I say *Se-len-a* slow and enunciate the Spanish
because when you say Selena in Spanish every
Tejana knows you're praying to the Queen of Tejano.
La Reina de Cumbia. Patron saint of red lipstick,
pizza, bombass bustiers, purple jumpsuits,
and washing machine hips. A voice untamed
by the American tongue. She's the patron saint
of Latinas everywhere: a light embossed into memory
that we can be something more in this borderland
of tongues. On this American soil so quick to tie
our names down to English—because don't you know
Selena Gomez was named after Selena. America
turned her into something it could hold in its mouth.

Portrait of a Father and his Daughters in Suburbia

Our ears were in tune
to the garage door rising,
the clatter of the back gate's

latch, and the doorknob's dance.
Our yells ran down the hallway
as we pushed each other out

of the way to greet you first.
Our arms twisting into a body's
hello, into a wordless: *I missed*

you Dad. A workday evening ritual.
The kind of tumble between two
daughters you let love itself into

the corners of the home. A chorus
always waiting for you at the end
of the day—when did the music

of laughter against windows quiet?
Do you remember the first night
we grew into an empty room?

Let the garage door close, the latch
mumble, the doorknob dance alone
—stopped calling out your name?

The Poet at Fifteen
after Erika L. Sánchez

Smoking weed, skipping class,
vodka in water bottles, sneaking
out at night—could earn me 15
beltings. But when my mother
found out I ditched the bus
to ride to school with a senior guy
from down the street—the bricks
in our house began to chatter,
stifling smoke and ready
to burn flesh. Her question

Who are you fucking?

given as a sentence. My voice
responded with *No one* but her
mind had cemented me into a liar.
I was already a slut tailing mis primas.
Their Corona dipped steps. Their one-
night slip-ups and knock ups. Girls
losing a game we were never asked
to play but the world's eye keeps
turning us chingada if we breathe
the same air. Our home split

Mentirosa.

like my mother imagines my legs
to be; like her mother did and hers.
My mother ready to drag the chingada
in me by the hair to a doctor's office

—to check if mi virginidad was still
intact. If it wasn't—I should be ready
for her to burn the bones she formed
in her womb because the worst her
own blood could do was embarrass
her in front of all the other mothers.

The Summer My Cousin Grew Taller than Me

The coats begin to fear the dark
heat of his breath. He wants to know
what a burning body tastes like

and my flame is the only one
within reach—a telenovela flickers
on the television. Dr. Pepper cans

are wet. Outside the dog's chain runs
along the dirt. The house empty of adults.
I become a whisper of a match

as my cousin leaves charred edges. The closet
opens to breathe. Abuela's shoes are crooked,
and a coat's shoulder hangs off the hanger

The Abortion My Mother Told Me Not to Write About

My Partner Asks if I Can Buy Him a New Belt

At Macy's I stand in front of the belt rack—all of them hang
like tongues. Their flesh hued from dirt to oak tree to night.
I cannot bring myself to touch them. An employee asks
if I need help—but I am already walking down the hallway
to my parents' bedroom. My hand against the wall feels
every bump until I stand in their closet. My mother waits
as I stare into the eyes of my father's belts. Four: one
braided. One thick, glossy, the color of coffee. Another thin
and the color of a desk. The other a dull night. I press them
between my fingers to decide which one would hurt the least
—but I know they can sing about pain. They will all count
my age—remind me of how old I have become. Remind me
of how I should know better. Remind me to clean my room,
to listen, to do as I'm told, to tell the truth, to come home
on time, to not trust boys, to not talk back. They will remind
me of the strength in my mother's arm. They will remind her
of her own beltings, that this is the only way—a prayer—

to keep us protected.

Hands of Mothers

Bless the hands whirlpooling
sunshine into our backs.

The ones pulling our bodies
through the small pains

of lost toys and friends.
The hands that may have

never planned on being
a mother and the ones

that feared being enough.
Bless the hands of mothers

who never had one to follow.

Returning to the Moment I Learned To Count

my imperfections: in our small house
        in Houston, my two hands swollen
and puffy from rips of skin,
        my six-year-old fingernails bitten.

Each time my fingers seek the comfort
        of my mouth you slap them,
rub jalapeño pepper juice into the cuts
        then cover them with gloves. Seven

brings new glasses: you hand me
        the pretty bronze frame and I jump
from the clearer vision of the parking lot.
        I smile until you introduce me

to the word four-eyes. At ten I struggle
        to fix my short hair, smooth the dark mess
into a half ponytail before school. But it's ugly:
        you pull the chongo out. You call attention

to the smell of my puberty, to the stains heavy
        on denim and pads in need of a change
because *I smell like vagina*. Fifteen: I run
        around the pool with cousins until you say

my stomach pouch makes me look
        pregnant. I wrap myself in a pale yellow
beach towel. At seventeen, I need
        to wax my eyebrows. At twenty-two, I still

don't wear makeup. At twenty-four, I need
        more exercise. At twenty-five, I need newer
clothes, makeup, and still more exercise. At twenty-six,
        I understand how life has claimed you.

Notes on Absence
Houston, Texas

3

4

1

2

5

1 In photos, my mother's life began at sixteen. One: she stands beside
        Sears co-workers in fur coats with her hands on her hips.
    Two: short hair permed, high waist jeans against an '82 Honda.
Three: a glamour shot, black leather held up to her left cheek.

2 The photos don't smell like Dove or hairspray. They don't smell
        like Estée Lauder's Beautiful on date nights. When I walk
    through a Macy's I remember gold lipstick tubes and a few
smudges on my bottom lip. 3 I would get in trouble if I wasn't careful

with the family albums. I was always in trouble. 4 We have a studio
        print of my father as a baby—a blue onesie—the one framed
    on my abuela's wall. There is no baby photo of my mother
hanging on her mother's wall. Did I even ask once about her baby

photo? Or worse, did she walk away and cry the day I asked *Where
        are you? Why don't you have baby pictures?* Did she answer
    and I just forgot? 5 My mother was forty-eight when a cousin
uploaded a black and white photo: my mother on the far left

in her baby dress, her sister beside her, and three older brothers
        in checkered shirts. The soles of their shoes exposed
    and worn. No time stamp. No cursive to examine on the back.
But I can see myself, in this 4x6, in her outstretched fingers.

Portrait of a Daughter and her Mother on the Sidewalk
after Ada Limón

Bare feet and a sunflower

dress, she stood

beside her mother

on the sidewalk, under

a tree at six years old.

Before her baby was born.

      she moved an ocean away.

      they became strangers.

      they stopped talking.

      the broken ceramic spoon.

      the divorce.

      she returned

from Mexico with no room

left to hold her mother's pain.

Before the land between them

split and she grew brave

enough to save the child,

she once was, from the house

that belonged to her mother.

She never knew

how it would feel

to be mothered.

Who La Llorona's Daughter Cries For

I see the two blue lines

> as doves made of dusk's dew.

Thirty-two and pregnant.

The two blue lines hum before overflowing into song,
    piano keys for my in-laws: *Your son will be*
                                                a father.

I think of my mother.

Throughout the next nine months, I wonder
    if my mother sat inside the tub
        too sick to eat. I want to ask
            how she carried a pond in her belly.

            Did she feel like a forgotten melody?

In the delivery room, I don't call for my mother:
    I tumble low
        over and over like earth
            surrendering to the stream.

            Every contraction,
                    a welcome, an undoing,

    a promise:
            not to become my mother,
                    a broken child,

a woman unable to forgive
a world that took her mother.

In those first seconds my child comes up for breath

I call for no one.

Repeat After Me

Today I will be the water
        when the laundry room floods

                at 3 am. The wind under a palm
        counting the trees as it drives by.

Today I will be the thorned tears
    in the window screen. The dead

branches in my mother's garden
    of rosas. The receipts in her purse.

Today I will be the steady grind
        of a molcajete. Accidental burns

                gifted by the comal. Memories
        of scars, blisters, and silence.

Today I will be an old Mazz song
    on cassette. The last couple norteña-ing

in an emptied dance hall. A busted stereo.
    Cervezas clustered in the center of tables.

Today I am Amanda. I am
        the meaning of my name:

                I am worthy. I am worthy.
        I am worthy of love—today.

Acknowledgements

An abundance of gratitude to the readers and editors of the following publications in which earlier versions of these poems first appeared:

The Acentos Review: "Returning to the Moment I Learned to Count," "First Time I Interrupted Mamá Talking," "Where is my Mexican Mother?"

The Boiler Journal: "DFW to LAX," "Before I Was Born," and "When I Ask My Brother About Our Dad"

Harpur Palate: "The Poet at Fifteen"

Huizache: "The First Language," "CPS," and "Mamá in the Cotton Fields"

Hypertext Magazine: "My Mother's Words" and "Empty Bottles and Beer Cans"

Puerto del Sol: "The Abortion My Mother Told Me Not to Write About"

RHINO Poetry: "You Have to Be Ready"

Rust + Moth: "Enough"

The Shallow Ends: "Tongue Untethered"

Silk Road Review: "When The Weather Changes" and "The Summer My Cousin Grew Taller than Me"

TAYO Literary Magazine: "Elegy for the Migrant Worker's Hands," "The Songs of Brujería," "The Nurse" and "Who La Llorona Cries For"

The Texas Review: "Where My Umbilical is Buried"

Up the Staircase Quarterly: "When My Little Sister Mistakes Selena for Selena Gomez"

Watershed Review: "Cicada Shells" and "Absence Forgotten"

Waxwing Magazine: "Letter to my First Gold Hoops" and "My Partner Asks if I Can Buy Him a New Belt"

Whurk: "Notes on Absence"

Songs of Brujería, a short chapbook containing several of these poems, was published by Big Lucks in 2019.

Thank You

A hundred thank yous to the organizations that have supported me on the way: Storyknife, MacDowell, Monson Arts, Voices of Our Nation Arts Foundation, Vermont Studio Center, Sewanee Writers' Conference, Sundress Academy for the Arts, New York State Summer Writers Institute, Robert Rauschenberg Foundation, Community of Writers, Virginia Center for the Creative Arts, The Muse Writers Center, and the MFA Program at Old Dominion University.

To my mentors and faculty who have given me guidance on this writing journey—Craig Santos Perez, Kristiana Kahakauwila, Noʻu Revilla, Cornelius Eady, Luisa A. Igloria, Tim Seibles, Tim Richardson, and Laura Kopchick. Thank you for hearing me. I hope to be as wonderful and generous as you one day.

To my Storyknife family, VONA family, VSC family, Community of Writers family, Fish House Crew, and GR8s—thank you for the wisdom, validation, late nights filled with real talks, warm cookies, and the life-giving inspiration.

To my writing and art friends—Michelle Moncayo, Sara Borjas, Anthony Cody, Mai Der Vang, Kay Ulanday Barrett, Mae Ramirez, Kei Kaimana, Addie Tsai, Emily Yoon, Sebastián Páramo, Mike Soto, Stephanie Adams-Santos, Alyssa Songsiridej, ire'ne lara silva, José Angel Araguz, Amanda Tachine, Heather Aruffo, Preeti Kaur, Violeta Orozco, Javier Gutiérrez Lozano, Mahogany L. Browne, Rachel Eliza Griffiths, Kat Hall, Kelsey Kerr, Emily Howell, Michael Alessi, and Cheryl Kutcher. Thank you for your friendship, laughter, love, food, art, and all the light you bring to this world. I'm grateful to share space with you and to cheer you on in all your endeavors. You continue to inspire me.

To Tenni, Tierney, and the wonderful team at Sundress—
whew. It's been a journey. Thank you for your patience, your
understanding, and for sticking with me. I am grateful for all
the care it has taken to bring this collection into the world.

A mi familia—gracias por su paciencia, for your endurance and
your resilience in a world that told you: You're not enough.
Gracias for allowing me to be a witness to the fractured beauty
of our shared lives.

A mi hermanita—I wouldn't have survived this last year
without you or your punny self. Thanks for putting up with me.
I love you and I'm always proud of you.

To my first reader and kite string—Minh-Đức. El amor de mi
vida gracias por todo. Especialmente durante este último año
cuando I could not recognize the me in these poems. Thank
you for your patience, steadfastness, care, and for being you.
Thank you for witnessing this life—the good, the tough, the
mundane—and allowing me to be a part of yours. Em yêu anh.

A mi primer bebé, Ardin. El otro amor de mi vida—gracias for
choosing me to be your mama. I can't wait to watch your light
grow.

About the Author

Amanda Galvan Huynh (she/her) is a Chicana writer and educator from Texas. She is the author of a chapbook, *Songs of Brujería* (Big Lucks) and Co-Editor of *Of Color: Poets' Ways of Making: An Anthology of Essays on Transformative Poetics* (The Operating System). Her writing has been supported by fellowships and scholarships from MacDowell, Storyknife, Monson Arts, Robert Rauschenberg Foundation, Sewanee Writers' Conference, Virginia Center for the Creative Arts, and others.

Other Sundress Titles

Kneel Said the Night
Margo Berdeshevsky
$20

Little Houses
Athena Nassar
$12.99

In Stories We Thunder
V. Ruiz
$16

the Colored page
Matthew E. Henry
$16

Slack Tongue City
Mackenzie Berry
$16

Year of the Unicorn Kidz
jason b. Crawford
$16

Sweetbitter
Stacey Balkun
$16

Something Dark to Shine In
Inès Pujos
$16

Cosmobiological
Jilly Dreadful
$20

Slaughter the One Bird
Kimberly Ann Priest
$16

What Nothing
Anna Meister
$16

To Everything There Is
Donna Vorreyer
$16

Hood Criatura
féi hernandez
$16

nightsong
Ever Jones
$16

www.ingramcontent.com/pod-product-compliance
Lightning Source LLC
Chambersburg PA
CBHW031145090426
42738CB00008B/1223